KEEP WALKING

40 Days to Hope and Freedom after Betrayal

Lynn Marie Cherry

As Christian counselors, we have to admit, we were so afraid that this book would be full of quick fixes and easy answers—"Just read your Bible and listen to pastors' tapes three times and you will be fine"—a book that glosses over the utter devastation that comes with betrayal. Instead, we found a book about real pain, deep struggles, and an honest look at despair. Not only does Lynn understand and give voice to the pain that comes with betrayal, but she also gives practical steps to walk out each painful day—slowly, with the future unknown, until a few faint notes of a song of hope begin stirring in your heart. She gets it and she is reaching out with hope to those in the midst of devastation. We can't wait to get copies of this book to give to our clients who have experienced betrayal.

—**Brent and Janis Sharpe**, Licensed Marriage and Family Therapists

Keep Walking is the book you don't want to need, but when you need it you are so grateful it exists. Recently I had a friend who experienced a marital betrayal and being able to give her a copy of this book was a tangible and practical way to love her during this season.

—**Amy Young**, author of *Looming Transitions*

Lynn Cherry shares her journey of betrayal, progress, and hope in her powerful work, *Keep Walking: 40 Days to Hope and Freedom after Betrayal*. With a transparency and candidness that stay true without veering into vengefulness, Lynn openly reveals the wrestling of her heart and the lessons learned along the way as she moved from the initial shock of discovering her marriage was not what she thought to the transformation and healing that were awaiting her on the other side of a chasm of chaos. Lynn will encourage you, give you tools for the journey, speak faith into the dark places, and speak from a place not of theory but tangibility when it comes to relationship revolution.

—**Julie Lyles Carr**, author of *Raising an Original* and pastor of Life-Women at LifeAustin

When recovering from infidelity, the spiritual component is critical. *Keep Walking* provides a much-needed path for allowing God to become part of the recovery process.

—**Rick Reynolds**, LCSW, president and founder of AffairRecovery. com

What a brilliant, compassionate, and helpful resource *Keep Walking* is for all who are journeying through any type of betrayal! Lynn will capture your heart and bring the much-needed hope you are longing for. Her empathy, practical wisdom, and distinguished way of presenting God's timeless truth are just what the doctor ordered, bringing exactly what is needed to experience the freedom you desire. We believe your life, as well as countless lives, will be positively affected because of this devotional. Read . . . listen with your heart . . . participate with all you've got . . . because glorious change is on the way!

—**Rob and Laura Koke**, senior pastors of Shoreline Church

Lynn Cherry knows the power of small steps to full healing. Let her words of deep revelation and truth bring you hope and a road map out of darkness into light, one day at a time!

—**Lynette Lewis**, author, speaker, and business consultant

The amazing power of sharing our stories with one another is that it reminds us that we are not alone, and opens the door for hope and healing to enter our hearts. Lynn definitely achieves this in her book, *Keep Walking*. As she shares her own personal story with such honesty and raw emotion, you feel like she is gently taking your hand and walking with you through your own journey toward healing. It is full of life-giving Scripture and practical yet creative ways to reflect and respond to what the Holy Spirit is speaking to your heart as you read.

—**Ross and Aimee Parsley**, pastors of One Chapel

Keep Walking is real help for surviving the very real pain of betrayal. Lynn tells so many women's stories as she is telling her own. Reading this book is like having a conversation with a wise, close friend who knows you very well. She captures significant moments in the murky journey of restoration and expresses them in images that touch right where it hurts. This is solid, biblical counsel for gaining emotional and spiritual health from someone who has walked that path herself. It's very relatable and could also help those who have been through other types of devastating loss. This book would be a perfect tool for a small group setting on restoration.

—**Bonnie Fehlauer**, life group and women's pastor of New Life Church

Contents

Foreword

Betrayal. We cringe when we read the word, and yet we've all had to deal with it: in personal relationships, at work, among friends. Lynn Cherry has faced it as well, but she has triumphed over it with the Lord's help. Through this book you will learn from her journey and experience joy on the other side of betrayal.

How does one overcome betrayal? It's tough. Very tough. I wish I could say I had no firsthand knowledge of this, but every now and then I'm hit again. Sometimes from out of the blue. The Enemy knows just how to get his jabs in, and he is skilled in the art of manipulation. But when you know who you are in Christ, the lies (eventually) roll off of you. Oh, they try to stick, but truth triumphs a lie every time.

No matter what you're going through, be reminded of one thing: we have a Savior who understands. He was betrayed too—by those he loved, by the people who once claimed to love him. In spite of it all, Jesus chose to keep his head up and speak peace. Love. Hope. Ponder that, as you ask yourself, "Where is God in my pain? Doesn't he see what's happening to me? Doesn't he care?"

He's right there. He's been through it. He walked an agonizing road to the cross with lies being spewed all around him. Mocking. Tormenting. Jeering. And all from the same crowd of people who had cheered him on a week prior.

People can hurt us. They can turn on us. They can betray. But Jesus truly meant what he said when he spoke these amazing words:

"Blessed are the poor in spirit,
for theirs is the kingdom of heaven.
Blessed are those who mourn,

1

for they will be comforted.
Blessed are the meek,
  for they will inherit the earth.
Blessed are those who hunger
  and thirst for righteousness,
  for they will be filled.
Blessed are the merciful,
  for they will be shown mercy.
Blessed are the pure in heart,
  for they will see God.
Blessed are the peacemakers,
  for they will be called children of God.
Blessed are those who are persecuted
  because of righteousness,
  for theirs is the kingdom of heaven.

"Blessed are you when people insult you, persecute you and falsely say all kinds of evil against you because of me. Rejoice and be glad, because great is your reward in heaven, for in the same way they persecuted the prophets who were before you" (Matt. 5:3–12).

You are not alone. You are not without hope. Ponder these things as you're reading through Lynn Cherry's wonderful book. Let her journey prompt you to find freedom from bitterness and pain. May you be set free as you read!

—Janice Thompson, author of the Weddings by Bella series

Introduction

I work at a church and a couple years ago after the teenagers returned from summer camp, an unclaimed suitcase stood abandoned near my cubicle. I knew that thing was filled with some teenager's damp, dirty, disgusting camp clothes, and I was not about to touch it. I had already dealt with the mess my own two boys brought home from camp, and that was enough for me.

The suitcase sat near my cubicle for months. No one came to claim it. No one missed it. It was almost as if it didn't exist.

I know all about packing things away and pretending they don't exist.

After a few decades on the planet, this is how I learned to deal with unpleasant circumstances and emotions. If it didn't fit my lovely-life plan, I stuffed it inside, pretended it hadn't happened, and all was well.

I brought this habit, this pattern—this baggage—into my marriage.

My husband brought his own baggage.

Like so many young men, he grew up with pornography. It was the one vice that maintained a grip on his life even after he gave his heart to Jesus.

I had no idea it was a part of his world. It came to light slowly over several years. As I learned about it, I did what I did best: I stuffed and pretended.

So my husband brought porn baggage. I brought stuffing-and-pretending baggage. We had no idea our life luggage coordinated so well! It was a matching set, a ticking time bomb of his-and-hers dirty laundry.

Our mutual brokenness worked for a long time, nearly six years.

It wasn't until I was an anxious, angry woman that I finally got fed up with my flawed coping strategies and reached out for help.

I realized at the first couples' therapy session my husband and I attended that I was the biggest basket case in the bunch. Seriously. I cried more, whined more, and soaked more tissues than anyone else. It was humiliating.

I went home that day determined to find some measure of healing. I hoped, at the very least, that I would be able to hold it together during the next session. Thankfully I knew where to go. I found real help, comfort, and courage in the Bible.

Soon, I had passages written on sticky notes everywhere—in the pantry, on my bathroom mirror, in my wallet, and on the dashboard of the minivan. Keeping these sacred words in front of me helped me move forward. If all you see right now is the murky blackness of betrayal, it might sound too good to be true. But it is true. And what happened for me can happen for you too.

Here is the reality: in the darkness I couldn't see how or even if I would make it out alive. But the Word of God really was a lamp unto my feet, helping me see each next step. When all I wanted to do was curl up in a corner and cry the day away, these words from the Bible were like a warm blanket wrapping me up in mind-boggling peace and giving me the courage to crawl out of my corner and face another day.

The pain of betrayal decimated me. I became an empty shell of a woman, but I am no longer that broken girl. Jesus restored my soul one small step at a time.

The thoughts and Scriptures compiled in this 40-day devotional carried me through my personal wilderness. I encourage you to look for your own lifelines and grab hold of them.

If you're like me, you might be tempted to read through this book in one afternoon—and you easily could—but I encourage you to slow down. Take time to reflect. Grab a notebook and respond to the questions. Let each affirmation become your mantra for one single day.

On the other side of the pain of betrayal, there is hope and there is freedom. Just keep walking and you will make it through.

—Lynn

Day 1

You Are Not Alone

As our first couples' counseling session wrapped up, we were each handed a survey to complete and turn in on our way out of class. I can still see the last question on the bottom right-hand corner of the page:

circle one: Betrayed   or   Betrayer

After years of coping with denial, circling the word "Betrayed" was an ah-ha moment with a bite, but it was the beginning of help for me. I had been betrayed by my husband. He battled a secret life of addiction to pornography, and I was a casualty of that war.

The pain and brokenness of that moment were penetrated by one thought: I'm not the only one. I remembered a simple phrase quoted often during communion services: "on the night he was betrayed" (1 Cor. 11:23). Those words spoke solidarity.

Jesus had lived this moment. He had suffered this pain. Judas walked with Jesus as his disciple for three years and then betrayed him with the intimacy of a kiss. I wasn't alone in this feeling or this experience.

You are not alone either.

The disappointment, the tears, the anger, and the fear are a human response to human suffering. Today I want to remind you that the Word became flesh. Jesus is Emmanuel, God with us. He walked this earth in human form, and he knows how it feels to be betrayed by those closest to you.

When Jesus walked our dusty roads and saw the hurting people around him, he was moved with compassion. Maybe it was our shared humanity that moved him so. My prayer for you today is that you will feel his compassion wash over your own flesh and bone, that you will know you are never alone.

Today I will remember I am not alone.

Reflect and Respond:

"And be sure of this: I am with you always, even to the end of the age" (Matt. 28:20 NLT).

Imagine Jesus standing with you, moved with compassion, in the moment you discovered you had been betrayed. Feel his nearness.

If Jesus could write you a letter, what might he say about your experience as someone who has also felt the sting of betrayal?

Day 2

Loved by God

For years after our wedding day, my husband continued calling me his bride. It was quite endearing. However, when his struggle with pornography came to light, it felt like sandpaper on my soul.

One evening at church when I walked into worship rehearsal, he yelled across the room, "There's my bride."

Another guy on the team turned to me and asked, "How does it feel to be loved like that?"

I don't remember responding, although I'm sure I stumbled through an acknowledgement of sorts. I do remember thinking, how can he call me his bride and continue to trample on my heart?

It's hard to understand, but in David's mind his pornography use was unrelated to how he felt about me and our marriage. He stuffed the two topics in different boxes in his brain, and the two boxes never touched. He never stopped loving me, but his words lost their power to convince me of his love.

I felt devalued, rejected, and unworthy. I wasn't enough for him. That pornography box toppled over, rolled out of its place in his world, and crushed mine.

We all need to feel loved and valued. Tragically, sometimes the people we most need to feel loved by are the ones who betray our hearts.

The love of family and friends can help ease the pain, but the only love that sweeps up the flattened, broken pieces and puts them back together is the unending, unconditional, unfathomable love of God.

God wrapped his tender arms around me with this verse from

the book of Isaiah: "Since you are precious and honored in my sight, and because I love you . . ." (Isa. 43:4).

You are precious and honored in God's eyes. You are loved by the Creator of the universe. He sees you. He knows you. He loves you.

You are deeply and dearly loved.

Loved. Valued. Accepted. Worthy. Enough.

Today I will remember I am loved by God.

Reflect and Respond:

If you ever doubt God's love, all you have to do is look to the cross.

"For God so loved the world that he gave his one and only Son" (John 3:16).

"This is love: not that we loved God, but that he loved us and sent his Son as an atoning sacrifice for our sins" (1 John 4:10).

Spend some time reflecting on God's love displayed on the cross. Watch a movie about Jesus. Write a thank-you note to God acknowledging his actions as a gift of extravagant love for you.

"And I pray that you, being rooted and established in love, may have power, together with all the Lord's holy people, to grasp how wide and long and high and deep is the love of Christ, and to know this love that surpasses knowledge" (Eph. 3:17–19).

Did you notice the phrase "together with all the saints"? We come to know the expanse of God's love in community. Ask a friend to tell you how she knows she is loved by God.

Day 3

Hope Paints a Thin Pink Line

Recently I was up early taking my son to football practice before school. As I watched the sunrise transform the sky, I remembered my own personal darkness. I remembered days when it seemed unlikely that light would ever shine again.

Rummaging through old notes and journals, I found an entry that shocked me. Our family had taken a trip to the coast. I got up early one morning, sat on the balcony, and thought about grabbing my flip-flops for a walk on the beach. The thought crossed my mind to walk out into the waves and never turn back. I was already drowning in pain; it seemed fitting. It wasn't a safe place for me.

Maybe you find yourself surrounded by darkness. Drowning. You can't see a way out. You can't see your own hand in front of your face. I've been there and I remember.

Before the light ever broke through, God was with me in the dark.

One of the tenets of the Christian faith is God's omnipresence. He is always present, with us in darkness just as much as in light. It can be hard to feel his nearness in the dark. Jesus called out from the cross, "'My God, my God, why have you forsaken me?'" (Matt. 27:46). Jesus felt alone, forsaken in the darkness of that moment. But Jesus was not alone. "For God was in Christ, reconciling the world to himself" (2 Cor. 5:19 NLT). God was there with Jesus all along, and he is with you right now no matter how dark your situation may seem.

The danger in forgetting our times of darkness is we trivialize coming into the light. We forget how slowly and stubbornly darkness relinquishes its hold on the night. Hope paints a very thin pink line. If you are not watching closely, you may miss its initial glow.

Hope rises in our hearts at different tempos. Sometimes it pops right up. A one, and a two, and a three, and BOOM. Brilliance! At other times, darkness shrouds hope like thick black molasses and the sunrise drags on like a funeral dirge. It took years for hope to rise glorious in my life, to revive my heart.

I have lived in darkness. But I know without a doubt that light shines. Every morning we see this truth on display.

Hope paints the sky in thin pink lines
    blooming orange
    bursting yellow
    bright.
The heavens declare it
    clear in phosphorus hue
    today and each new day
    darkness loses to Light.

Today I will watch for thin pink lines of hope.

Reflect and Respond:

"'Because of God's tender mercy, the morning light from heaven is about to break upon us, to give light to those who sit in darkness and in the shadow of death, and to guide us to the path of peace'" (Luke 1:78–79 NLT).

Wake up early tomorrow and watch the sunrise.

Describe what you see and how you feel. Take a picture and save it as the wallpaper on your phone.

Get some colored pencils, watercolors, or scrapbooking supplies and create a sunrise scene. Put it on your nightstand for those mornings you aren't up before the sun.

If you are dealing with suicidal thoughts, please tell someone immediately. Call the National Suicide Prevention Lifeline at 1-800-

273-8255.

"I have come as a light to shine in this dark world, so that all who put their trust in me will no longer remain in the dark" (John 12:46 NLT).

Day 4

God Sees

Deep in space there is a vivid reminder of a God who sees it all. The Helix Nebula, as captured by the Hubble Space Telescope, is often referred to as the Eye of God. One morning, I opened my email and a friend had sent a picture of the Helix Nebula with a simple but profound message, God sees.

God sees you. He sees your tears. He sees how you have been hurt. He sees it all. He sees us all.

Hagar was the maidservant of Sarai, Abram's wife. She was caught in the middle of the long-awaited promise for a son. When Sarai got impatient with God, she took matters into her own hands. She gave her maidservant to her husband Abram, and Hagar became pregnant. How that ever seemed like a solution or a realization of the promise is beyond me. There was very little love in Hagar's corner of the love triangle. Before long, Sarai turned on her and mistreated her. Then Abram abandoned her. Hagar took her son and ran away.

But God met her in that lonely place, and when he did, Hagar came to know him in a new way, by a new name.

"She gave this name to the Lord who spoke to her: 'You are the God who sees me,' for she said, 'I have now seen the One who sees me.' That is why the well was called Beer Lahai Roi" (Gen. 16:13–14). "Beer Lahai Roi" means, "well of the Living One who sees me." God became the life-giving spring in Hagar's desert.

I pray God will meet you in each lonely moment and remind you of his promise, that you will come to know him through this season in a new way and by a new name. He is the God who sees you.

Today I will remember God sees me.

Reflect and Respond:

Have you felt like running away? How is moving forward different from running away?

"Behold, I have indelibly imprinted (tattooed a picture of) you on the palm of each of My hands" (Isa. 49:16 AMPC).

Look at the palm of your hand. See how close you are to God's face. What does he see as he looks at you today?

"Where can I go from your Spirit? Where can I flee from your presence? If I go up to the heavens, you are there; if I make my bed in the depths, you are there. If I rise on the wings of the dawn, if I settle on the far side of the sea, even there your hand will guide me, your right hand will hold me fast" (Ps. 139:7–10).

Day 5

No More Pretending

I lost it one day in our group therapy session.

It was our turn to sit in the middle of the room and share our homework from the previous week. I was trying to squeeze words out of the vice grip around my throat, but they would not come until I forced them.

"Why is this so hard for me?"

Our therapist leaned back in his chair, popped a mint in his mouth, and answered, "It's hard for an ostrich to pull her head out of the sand."

Can you believe he called me an ostrich? That's just wrong! But he was right.

It was hard to own the reality of my life. It was far easier to pretend. I got pretty good at pretending. For six years I pretended. Six years of my life I spent on pause.

Looking at the problem and going to counseling every week was gut-wrenching. It was like a weekly scraping of my wound. I hated it. I wanted to quit, skip our lunch-hour session, and go out to eat instead.

But there is no real life in pretending—only existence, going through the motions, and not feeling much at all. Pretending provided some level of numbness to the pain, but we cannot selectively anesthetize only our bad feelings. In numbing myself to pain, I was also missing any joy that tried to come my way. Slowly, numbness pervaded every area of my life like a sticky black oil spill. I was stuck in a prison I created.

Say no to pretending. Pull your head out of the sand no matter

Keep Walking

how uncomfortable it is to open your eyes and really see what's
going on.

Pretending made a mannequin out of me. I may have looked
alive, but inside I was hollowed out by the pain I refused to acknowledge. That's no way to live. I hope my story will save you
from years of denial.

Today I will stop pretending.

Reflect and Respond:

"Therefore is my spirit overwhelmed *and* faints within me
[wrapped in gloom]; my heart within my bosom grows numb" (Ps.
143:4 AMPC).

Are you using anything unhealthy in an attempt to numb the
pain you've been feeling?

Are you prone to pretending?

We may feel safe within the walls of our pretending prisons,
but Jesus came to set us free.

"He has sent me to bind up the brokenhearted, to proclaim
freedom for the captives and release from darkness for the prisoners" (Isa. 61:1).

Sometimes it is easier for me to believe Jesus will heal me from
hurt that others have caused, but self-inflicted pain produced by my
own choices is mine to endure. Have you made that distinction in
processing your own pain?

Jesus wants you free whether you were imprisoned by others'
actions or walked right in and slammed the prison door yourself!

"So thank God for his marvelous love, for his miracle mercy
to the children he loves; He shattered the heavy jailhouse doors,
he snapped the prison bars like matchsticks!" (Ps. 107:15–16 The
Message).

Day 6

God Is a Good God

God was so faithful to speak to me during the trauma of owning my pain. Many times a song or a Scripture would pick me up and carry me through the day. Be on the lookout for love messages from your Savior. Play those songs over and over. Memorize those verses. Cement the words in your spirit.

Start with this:

"I would have despaired unless I had believed that I would see the goodness of the Lord in the land of the living" (Ps. 27:13 NASB).

The psalmist says, "I would have despaired." When devastation occurs, despair settles in. It becomes our default setting. But we break the hold of despair by believing our God is a good God. He loves you and he is for you.

I grew up watching Oral Robert's *Expect a Miracle* program on TV. I can picture my preteen self sitting on the green shag carpeting in front of our thirteen-inch black and white television. I see the TV singers in their polyester leisure suits and long floral dresses, and I hear them singing, "Something good is going to happen to you."

Would you have the courage to believe that something good is going to happen to you today?

Hope is the positive expectation of good. Believe you will see God's goodness in your life today.

God is good. No matter what life may throw at us, he has the power to turn things around. He heals. He restores. He saves. He redeems. He makes all things new.

Keep Walking

My prayer is that you will have eyes to see God loving you, that you will see his goodness in your life in some sweet way today.

Today I believe I will see
the goodness of the Lord toward me.

Reflect and Respond:

Say this out loud: "God, I believe I will see your goodness in my life. I believe I will see your goodness in my family. I believe I will see your goodness in my future. I believe something good is going to happen to me today."

"Whatever is good and perfect is a gift coming down to us from God our Father, who created all the lights in the heavens. He never changes or casts a shifting shadow" (James 1:17 NLT).

I trained myself to notice the everyday gifts of God's goodness after reading Ann Voskamp's *One Thousand Gifts: A Dare to Live Fully Right Where You Are*.[1] I began keeping my own list of daily gifts. Write down three things you are grateful for, good gifts coming to you from the Father. Consider keeping an ongoing list of ordinary gifts.

Day 7

Mostly Dead Slightly Alive

I expected another twenty-hour ordeal, but our second son was born just twenty minutes after we arrived at the hospital. It was such a rush! I felt powerful, like I could conquer the world, but my stay on the top of that mountain was short-lived.

The day after we brought him home from the hospital, I woke up for a midnight feeding. I swaddled my baby boy, laid his sweet head in the crib, and was heading back to bed when I noticed the light on in our home office. Grateful not to be the only grown-up awake in the middle of the night, I opened the door.

In an instant I felt sin's double whammy—the steamy enticement of lust followed by the suffocating oppression of shame. Over my husband's shoulder, I saw pornography on the computer screen.

I was devastated. The something's-not-quite-right I suspected for years was right there on the screen.

I began a slow process of dying that night. Every day, every month, every year thereafter I grew a little colder and a little deader.

I was the walking dead before zombies were cool. Shuffling through life. Barely existing. Going through the motions. Walking wounded.

One day, years into my life as the walking dead, I was watching *The Princess Bride* with my boys. I certainly didn't feel like a princess, but I could identify with Wesley laid out on the table with his friends leaning in, hoping for a miracle. Miracle Max picks up a bellows and forces air into Wesley's lungs. He tells Wesley's friends, "It just so happens that your friend here is only mostly dead. There's a big difference between mostly dead and all dead. Mostly dead is slightly alive."[2]

Ha! That was me—mostly dead but still slightly alive. And if you are reading this book right now, guess what? You are still alive! This is not the end of you.

Life and hope began to stir in me as I dug into God's word. His words are life.

"'And the very words I have spoken to you are spirit and life'" (John 6:63 NLT).

My Bible became the bellows that filled my lungs with clean, crisp life.

Hold on to the hope you find in the Word of God. Allow him to breathe life into the lifeless areas of your soul.

Today I choose life.

Reflect and Respond:

"'Today I have given you the choice between life and death, between blessings and curses. Now I call on heaven and earth to witness the choice you make. Oh, that you would choose life, so that you and your descendants might live!'" (Deut. 30:19 NLT).

Do you feel like the walking wounded? Or the walking dead?

What would it look like for you to choose life today? How would you benefit from that choice? How would others benefit?

Do something fun that energizes you and makes you feel alive.

"'This is my comfort *and* consolation in my affliction: that Your word has revived me *and* given me life'" (Ps. 119:50 AMPC).

Get a dry erase marker and write a life-giving Scripture on your bathroom mirror.

Day 8

Just Jesus and Me?

When I found out about my husband's pornography use, I was embarrassed and afraid. I was ashamed of what was happening in our home, and I thought if anyone at our church found out, David would be fired and maybe he should be.

My husband didn't want to be addicted to pornography. But he didn't want anyone to know about his secret life. He told himself, "Just Jesus and me, we can beat this."

That didn't work for him.

I've wondered why. I mean, it sure would have saved me a whole lot of heartache if he could have conquered it on his own.

I won't say I found the answer, but I will say I found a case study in the Old Testament. Aren't you glad there are very human, very flawed people in the Bible?

David was the King of Israel. He had several wives, but one day he decided he wanted another woman. Never mind the fact that she was already married to someone else. It's quite a story. David assumed he had gotten away with adultery, covered it up with murder, and went on with his life.

When the prophet Nathan visited David and told him the story of a man with plenty of sheep who took another man's cherished lamb, David was outraged. He gave the thief a death sentence. He had the power to do that.

His eyes were opened when Nathan revealed to David that he—King David himself—was the thief in the story.

It wasn't until another flesh-and-blood human being entered

his secret world that King David's own eyes saw what he had done. Confrontation and shared realization were the beginning of freedom for David.

Jesus is the answer. He is the way, the truth, and the life. He is hope and freedom. I believe it with all my heart. But I also believe, especially when it comes to shameful secrets, that Jesus brings freedom through relationships and accountability.

You may need to invite other people into your story. I encourage you to look for a professional counselor who specializes in sexual addiction. He or she will know how to best help the betrayed and the betrayer.

Even though it was my husband who struggled with sexual addiction, I carried a great deal of shame. Shame is like mold: it thrives in cold, dark places.

It's uncomfortable to talk about those things that cause shame, but it's exactly what we have to do to break free from the chains that keep us underground. Even if your spouse refuses to seek help, you can reach out for the help you need.

**Today I will give myself permission
to seek professional help.**

Reflect and Respond:

"Where there is no counsel, the people fall; But in the multitude of counselors there is safety" (Prov. 11:14 NKJV).

Read 2 Samuel 11 and 12. Which characters in the story do you identify with: King David, Bathsheba, Uriah, or Nathan? How?

Read Psalm 51. King David wrote this psalm after the prophet Nathan confronted him. He poured out his heart in poetic prayer. How has your heart been tarnished? Have you lost joy? Write your own version of Psalm 51.

"Create in me a pure heart, O God, and renew a steadfast spirit within me. Do not cast me from your presence or take your Holy

Spirit from me. Restore to me the joy of your salvation and grant me a willing spirit, to sustain me" (Ps. 51:10–12).

Day 9

When I Am Afraid I Will Not Be Afraid

As a child, I learned to fear fear, thanks to my elementary school interpretation of Job's dreadful story and his "what I feared has come upon me" (Job 3:25). I tried to resist, but fear often gained the upper hand and swept me away with worst-case scenarios.

As an adult, I worried about my husband, my boys, and my own heart and then held my breath as if the act of being afraid initiated self-fulfilling prophesies in the dark, corner closet of my imagination. I wore myself out worrying about what our lives would become after the betrayal until I found a tool for tackling fear.

"When I am afraid, I put my trust in you. In God, whose word I praise—in God I trust and am not afraid" (Ps. 56:3–4).

Isn't it interesting how the writer of this psalm says in verse 3, "When I am afraid," but then just a sentence later in verse 4, "I will not be afraid"? That's a pretty big shift, and it happens in only fifteen words. What takes place between the fear and no fear? Let me break it down.

"When I am afraid . . ." Inevitable, right? Fear is part of life on this planet. Sometimes it is the most appropriate emotional response. Fear is par for the course when you are facing betrayal. But left alone, fear can morph into crippling things like anxiety and panic.

"I put my trust in you . . ." This sounds like a conscious decision to me. It's like the author is saying, "When fear comes, I have a choice and I choose to trust."

"In God, whose word I praise . . ." God's Word is just the place to take our fear. In his Word we find hope, freedom, peace, and joy.

We read that God is faithful. He is strong. He is loving. He never changes. We find all kinds of reasons to praise him, and when we praise him, we take our eyes off of our circumstances and look up. Our perspective changes. He is the glory and the lifter of our heads!

"In God I trust . . ." The decision to trust happens before the praise. After the praise, the writer affirms in whom his trust lies: in the God of the Word, the God he just praised, the God who delivers and heals and restores. Our God is trustworthy!

"And am not afraid . . ." We choose to trust, we go to the Word, we lift our praise, we affirm the God who is worthy of trust, and that is when things change. The situation doesn't necessarily change, but we change. We are not swept away or captured or paralyzed any longer.

We don't have to give in to fear. We can choose trust and praise.

Today I will let fear remind me to trust.

Reflect and Respond:

What are you afraid of?

What is the worst thing that could happen?

Can you see God in the worst-case scenario?

"Trust God from the bottom of your heart; don't try to figure out everything on your own. Listen for God's voice in everything you do, everywhere you go; he's the one who will keep you on track" (Prov. 3:5–6 The Message).

I like to figure things out on my own. Trust is almost always a conscious decision I make only after fear scatters buckshot into my theories and plans. For every fear you mentioned above, find a Scripture and write a statement of trust in God.

Day 10

You Are Vulnerable

I did most of my crying in the shower. Maybe it's because that's one of the few places I got to be alone as a young mom. Maybe I felt safer knowing the falling water would camouflage my falling tears.

During one of my crying sessions, a thought crossed my mind: "Surely there is a man out there who would be satisfied with just me, who wouldn't need me AND pornography."

Thoughts like this eventually opened my eyes to my own vulnerability.

I started reading *When Godly People Do Ungodly Things* by Beth Moore in an effort to understand what was happening in my marriage.[3] My husband was a Bible school graduate working in full-time ministry. He loved God. How could he have a sexual addiction?

Through reading Beth's book, I realized how easy it is for any of us to fall into a web of deception. I was weak, easy prey. Thankfully God rescued me before the enemy could devour me. Her words found me just in time to help shore up my own boundaries.

As a woman walking through the heartache of betrayal, maybe you've dealt with ideas similar to my thoughts in the shower. Would you allow me to warn you? This is not the time to be searching for an old friend on Facebook or going out to lunch with a cute coworker.

You need accountability. Tell a wise friend, pastor, or counselor about your vulnerable position. Ask for help. Flee temptation or, better yet, avoid it all together.

It's one thing to process your spouse's sin; don't stack your own sin on top of that mess. It will only make recovery harder and longer.

**Today I will recognize my own vulnerability
and reach out for accountability.**

Reflect and Respond:

Take a good look at your relationships. Is there someone you are connecting with in a way that is not safe during this season of your life? Whom can you talk to safely about your situation? Contact that person today.

"No temptation has overtaken you except what is common to mankind. And God is faithful; he will not let you be tempted beyond what you can bear. But when you are tempted, he will also provide a way out so that you can endure it" (1 Cor. 10:13).

Being tempted is not a sin. Jesus was tempted. Write about a time when you felt tempted but looking back you can see how God provided a way out.

Day 11

You

"You" is a three-letter word we use every day. It's a simple pronoun that takes the place of a proper name. We often use this word to address groups of people. "How are you tonight?" or "It's good to see you." "You" may mean a bunch of friends or a room full of people.

That is how I have read this word in different passages of the Bible, but one day in the midst of our marriage crisis it sounded different.

Announcing the birth of Jesus, an angel told a group of shepherds, "'I bring you good news that will cause great joy...a Savior has been born to you'" (Luke 2:10-11).

Sure, I think the angel meant "you" as in "all y'all." (That's how we'd say it in Texas.)

Go ahead and hear "you" in the corporate sense now. A Savior has been born for all. For God so loved . . . the world.

Then pause, take a deep breath, and hear "you" as the very personal pronoun that it is.

Do YOU want help?

Do YOU long for hope?

Do YOU need rescue?

A Savior has been born to YOU. You matter.

Twenty chapters later, we see Jesus using this same little word just before his death.

"'This is my body given for you . . . This cup is the new covenant in my blood, which is poured out for you'" (Luke 22:19–20).

Sometimes it's easier to read this passage with a whole-world perspective, like a soft-focus lens on the price paid for me. When I read "you" as a private personal pronoun, I'm shocked and overwhelmed that I would be worth so much. Jesus is saying I am.

For all the times you feel like you are not worthy of love, Jesus is saying you are.

Jesus' body was broken for you, for the sin that separated you from God, and for the pain sin has caused.

Yes, he died for the "you" that encompasses all, but inside that word lies each precious soul, each cherished individual. See yourself in that word. You are worthy of great love and sacrifice.

**Today I will embrace salvation
in the most private, personal way.**

Reflect and Respond:

Read the following verses again, replacing "you" with your own name.

"'Do not be afraid. I bring you good news that will cause great joy for all the people. Today in the town of David a Savior has been born to _____; he is Christ the Lord'" (Luke 2:10–11).

"And he took bread, gave thanks and broke it, and gave it to them, saying, 'This is my body given for _____; do this in remembrance of me.' In the same way, after the supper he took the cup, saying, "This cup is the new covenant in my blood, which is poured out for _____" (Luke 22:19–20).

In what way do you need a Savior today?

Was it difficult to replace "you" with your own name? How?

Take communion, remembering Jesus' life poured out for you in the most personal, intimate sense.

Day 12

Own The Dot

I was comfortable in denial, camped out in my own private "pretend normal" and sitting in a session at Shine Women's conference. Christine Caine, our speaker, showed an image of a small black dot on a field of white.

Christine was born into pain, unwanted and unnamed as an infant, marginalized as a child, abused as a young woman. She knew all about dots. Her challenge for us was to try to see God in our future, bigger and more powerful than the dots in our past.

I looked up at the slide and was immediately drawn to all the white. I am so good at seeing the white.

"Whatever is pure, whatever is lovely, whatever is admirable— if anything is excellent or praiseworthy—think about such things" (Phil. 4:8).

I can do that all day! I have two healthy children. Food to eat. Clothes to wear. A lovely home to live in.

My mental list of white was rudely interrupted when that black dot popped off the screen and slapped me upside the head.

I HAVE A BLACK DOT?

This was not supposed to happen to me! Shaking my head, I tried to refocus, but it wouldn't go away. Slap! Sting! Sure enough, there it was in white and black. How could I have never noticed it before?

It seemed as if pretending about my life and ignoring my dot all those years allowed the dot to blind me. Like it was stuck on the end of my nose and everywhere I turned, everything I saw was shrouded by the dot I couldn't even acknowledge.

I knew it was time to pay attention, time to own my dot.

True confession: I used that Scripture in Philippians as an excuse for denial. And I was skipping the phrase "whatever is true."

We need to acknowledge what is true—what has happened and what is happening.

These dots on our lives will NOT be denied! The more I tried to deny the dot, the more it colored everything else in my world various shades of gray.

It is only after we own the dot that we are able to let it go.

Today I will own the dot that has marked my life.

Reflect and Respond:

In the classic 1965 movie *A Thousand Clowns*, Murray says, "You gotta own your own days and name 'em, each one of 'em, every one of 'em, or else the years go right by and none of them belong to you."[4]

What part of your reality are you afraid to own?

Make a list of the dots that have marked your life. Note whether the dots have been owned or denied.

What steps can you take to own your dots?

What is at stake if you keep pretending?

Are there dots you are clinging to and need to let go of?

For every dot on your list, write a statement of surrender and release.

Day 13

The Big Blowup

We were watching a movie in the living room when I caught a whiff of an all too familiar odor. Call it the Great Burned Popcorn Incident. Someone pressed an extra button on the microwave and we were popping popcorn for thirty minutes instead of three. You know the end of that story. We nearly took our microwave apart to clean each smell-stained crevice.

As I reached in and wiped gunk out of the blower, I realized we had lived in this house for a while now and I'm pretty sure we had never cleaned this before. A gooey substance had been collecting in there for years, and it would have continued to build up if it wasn't for the popcorn blowup.

It's not pretty but in some ways a relational blowup is a gift, because it forces us to deal with our messes. I pretended not to see the mess in our marriage for about six years. I closed my eyes. I looked away. I didn't want to be responsible for the reality of our lives. After stuffing those emotions for so long, things started coming out sideways.

My exploding emotions were an obvious clue that we needed help, so I called a counselor. We went to the appointment together in fear and trembling, neither of us knowing how the story would end.

My husband learned how to break the cycle of sin and shame. I learned to break free from pretending and denial. We both gained relational tools that equipped us to do the hard work of cleaning up the mess and rebuilding our shattered life.

I know it sounds crazy, but I am grateful for the blowup.

Keep Walking

Be brave and let your blowup moments remind you that now is the time to get your hands dirty and begin the process of cleaning up the mess. There is a way through whatever you are facing.

**Today I will let the blowups motivate me
to start the clean up.**

Reflect and Respond:

When we finally started to get help, I was tormented by regret. Why didn't we get help sooner? What made me think pretending was a good option? What if I would have had the courage to confront the problem years ago?

Regret keeps you stuck in the past. Allow regret to remind you to repent. Turn from old familiar coping mechanisms and do the work.

"For God says, 'At just the right time, I heard you. On the day of salvation, I helped you.' Indeed, the 'right time' is now. Today is the day of salvation" (2 Cor. 6:2 NLT).

Today is the day. Now is the time. What one brave thing can you do today?

Day 14

Keeping My Eyes on Jesus

The ground began to give way, and she felt herself sliding off the cliff to the rocks and waves below.

"Look at me! LOOK AT ME!" Her friend held her hand but insisted on her gaze.

You've seen the scene played over and over on the big screen in slightly different settings with a wide variety of characters.

In a moment of fear and panic, what you focus on matters.

Maybe you can relate to this portion of an email I sent to a friend: "If I look at life in general right now, I get depressed. If I focus on my husband, I get mad. If I look at myself, I'm embarrassed and confused."

I know there is a lot going on, in and around you. When my husband and I began to deal with the issue in our marriage, all hell broke loose. Things went from bad to what-on-earth-is-happening worse. It felt like our relationship was falling to its doom, and we were sliding off the cliff right along with it.

Do you feel that way today?

Picture Jesus with a firm grasp on you, holding you steady but directing you intently, "Look at me."

Look.

At.

ME.

The chaos around you is not too much for him. The weight of all that is dragging you down is not too heavy. He has a hold on you. Keep your eyes set on him.

Keep Walking

Today I will keep my eyes focused on Jesus.

Reflect and Respond:

If you ever need help finding words to describe how you feel, check out Dr. Gloria Willcox's Feelings Wheel.[5] Choose two feelings from the wheel as you answer each question.

How do you feel about your life in general?

How do you feel about your spouse?

How do you feel about yourself?

"We do this by keeping our eyes on Jesus, the champion who initiates and perfects our faith. Because of the joy awaiting him, he endured the cross, disregarding its shame. Now he is seated in the place of honor beside God's throne" (Heb. 12:2 NLT).

You know those people who slow down when they drive by an accident on the highway? We call them rubberneckers. They often cause subsequent accidents because they stop looking where they are going. How can you remind yourself to keep your eyes on Jesus instead of staring helplessly at the wreckage in your life?

"If I keep my eyes on God, I won't trip over my own feet" (Ps. 25:15 The Message).

Day 15

Grieving

During our first twelve weeks of counseling, a precious family member experienced the tragic loss of a child. I flew out of state to be with her. Many family members gathered to grieve this painful loss together. As I watched family and friends rally around the shell-shocked parents, the pain felt so familiar it caught me off guard. I realized I was grieving.

I had lost the marriage I thought I had. I lost the fairy tale I once believed in. I lost hope for our future.

So much is lost in the wasteland of betrayal.

Are you grieving?

In her classic book *On Grief and Grieving*, Elisabeth Kübler-Ross presents five stages of loss:[6]

1. Denial and Isolation
2. Anger
3. Bargaining
4. Depression
5. Acceptance

Can you relate? Looking back I see myself bouncing back and forth like a pinball among stages one through four. Denial was the salve I slathered on my wounds for six years. Bargaining looked like buying lingerie in a failed attempt to compete with online images. Depression was like a weighted blanket that held me in bed too long. Anger was me hiding in the bathroom behind closed doors so I could curse and swear away from tiny ears. Acceptance was too hard to come by, so I steered clear of that stage.

The beauty in the ashes of my family member's loss was the

support and love that surrounded them. They were never alone. They were held.

I hope you are not alone as you navigate through grief's winding way. I hope there is a friend to hold you when you need to cry, someone to listen when you need to vent. I hope you are planted in a life-giving church that celebrates the power of the cross, the redemption of grace, and the value of relationships.

Pray about sharing your grief with a friend. Remember Psalm 34:18: "The Lord is close to the brokenhearted and saves those who are crushed in spirit."

May you sense his nearness today.

Today I will allow myself to grieve.

Reflect and Respond:

What have you lost?

What stages of grief have you experienced? Where do you see yourself right now?

Where have you turned for comfort?

"And I will pray the Father, and he shall give you another Comforter, that he may be with you forever. . . . But the Comforter, even the Holy Spirit, whom the Father will send in my name, he shall teach you all things, and bring to your remembrance all that I said unto you" (John 14:16, 26 ASV).

"'Blessed are those who mourn, for they will be comforted'" (Matt. 5:4).

Invite the Holy Spirit to be your Comforter.

Day 16

I Am So Angry

I could tell something was wrong the minute I walked in the door. I was unpacking my suitcase when my husband confessed to relapsing while I was out of town. Part of me was thankful for his honesty, but the other part was furious. I had the sudden urge to throw my shoes at him. But why bother? What damage would flip-flops do?

I thought about throwing things a lot. I was so angry.

Often when people introduce me, they use words like "sweet" and "kind." Anger is out of character for me. But it got so bad that I started swearing. I'd never sworn in my life! I would close the door to our bedroom, close the door to our bathroom, close the door to the little toilet room, and let the ugly, angry words loose.

I read the story of Jesus overthrowing the tables in the temple, and somehow I felt understood. The merchants in the temple yard were shortchanging the people who came to worship. They were cheating them, robbing them, betraying them. I was not alone in my anger.

Looking back I see my anger as a gift. Who knows how long I would have stayed stuck without anger to wake me up out of my sleep-like state of denial.

Are you angry? Don't condemn yourself for feeling that way. You have a valid reason for anger.

Anger is typically a secondary emotion. It follows on the heels of other feelings. So look for the primary emotions under the surface of your anger. Are you sad? Lonely? Tired? Stressed?

The truth is I was okay being sad. I was okay being lonely. Sure, I was tired and stressed. But the anger scared me. I knew I had to do something. My increasing anger was what finally motivated me to get help.

Psalm 4:4 says, "Be angry and do not sin. Meditate within your heart on your bed, and be still" (NKJV).

Don't stew in your anger, but do pay attention. Take some time tonight to search your heart and be silent.

**Today I will allow my anger to be the catalyst
for growth and change.**

Reflect and Respond:

In Ephesians 4:26, Paul quotes Psalm 4:4 with added emphasis, "'In your anger do not sin': Do not let the sun go down while you are still angry." When we were first married I thought this passage meant that we had to resolve each and every conflict before our heads hit the pillows. Imagine two exhausted, emotionally flooded people trying to solve their problems at 2 am. It is helpful to separate releasing anger from resolving conflict. When emotions are high sometimes it is better to take a break and come back to the issue after you've gotten some rest.

I prefer the Psalmist's advice, it is much less volatile. It may take a while for you to quiet your heart and really be still. Practice few minutes of silence right now.

It is important that you find a safe way to dissipate anger. Here are some suggestions: Punch a pillow. Call a friend who will listen to you vent. Type a letter you will never send in all caps. Go for a run. Actually any form of exercise is a great place to start.

Day 17

Take Courage

Our children were small when we hit rock bottom. There were many mornings it was hard to get out of bed. I remember our boys climbing in bed with me and driving their Matchbox cars around the comforter and down the hill I made with my knees. They were a gift of life straight from God. I got out of bed for them.

Looking back I can see I had given up a life for myself, but I still wanted a future and a family for my children.

I would have lingered longer under the covers, hiding in the shadows of despair if it wasn't for those two little boys. Like the cowardly lion, I needed some courage—average, ordinary, everyday courage.

"Be strong and let your heart take courage, all you who wait for *and* hope for *and* expect the Lord!" (Ps. 31:24 AMPC).

I kept that passage on the dashboard of my Honda Odyssey for years. I love the action of it. Let your heart take courage. As if courage is out there within our grasp and all we have to do is reach out and grab hold of it.

Will you do that? Reach out? Take courage!

Don't worry, our strength, our courage does not rest solely in our own power. We wait for and hope for and expect the Lord. Our hope and expectation is only in him.

Wait. Hope. Expect Jesus to show up when you need him most. It's what he does.

One day his disciples were in a boat during a storm, and Jesus came walking on the water. They were afraid. I'd be afraid too. I often felt afraid in the weeks and months we spent in therapy.

Here's what is so beautiful about our Savior: he doesn't ridicule his disciples for their fear. He responds immediately and says, "Take courage. It is I. Do not be afraid" (Matt. 14:27 NASB).

Hear Jesus saying that to you today.

Today I will take courage.

Reflect and Respond:

Jesus walked right into the middle of the storm that his disciples were facing. He is with you in your storm. If you were in the boat with Jesus' disciples when he said, "Take courage," how would you have responded?

"We can rejoice, too, when we run into problems and trials, for we know that they help us develop endurance. And endurance develops strength of character, and character strengthens our confident hope of salvation. And this hope will not lead to disappointment. For we know how dearly God loves us, because he has given us the Holy Spirit to fill our hearts with his love" (Rom. 5:3–5 NLT).

Has hope ever led to disappointment in your life? How is the hope of salvation different?

Is there something you've always dreamed of doing but have been afraid to try? What is a practical way you can take courage today?

Day 18

Unpacking

Remember the suitcase I mentioned in the introduction? I waited for weeks, but no one called looking for a missing suitcase.

I decided that scary thing had to be opened up if it was ever to be returned to its owner. I enlisted a coworker to help me because I wasn't about to do it alone.

You may be tempted to hide your baggage and never let it see the light of day. There may be days when you'd like to unpack your dirty laundry and toss it on the boulevard where everyone would see it. When it comes to unpacking, your best bet is to enlist a few trusted friends who will help you through the process and keep you moving forward.

I was blessed to have some wonderful friends who helped me unpack our life luggage.

A dear friend watched the boys while David and I went to our group sessions. Many times when I returned from class I would plop on her sofa and relive the horror of that day's class: how they poked at my wound and how I blubbered. She is the most gracious listener I know and quick on the draw with a tissue. Processing our group therapy sessions with her helped me work through the pain and own our story.

On the days when I went straight to work after therapy, my coworker and I would make a quick lap around the building to hash out what happened in that day's session. She wasn't afraid to get dirty. She unzipped my pain without hesitation and helped me unpack the musty, moldy baggage I had stuffed away for years.

I had our Associate Pastor's contact in my favorites. I would call her in my desperate moments and imagine her looking at the caller ID saying, "Oh no, not Lynn again." But she kept picking up. She prayed with me and steered me away from my old familiar coping mechanisms. And she didn't judge me for swearing.

I don't know how I would have made the journey without these girls. I hope you don't have to unpack alone.

**Today I will reach out to a trusted friend
to help me unpack my baggage.**

Reflect and Respond:

"A person standing alone can be attacked and defeated, but two can stand back-to-back and conquer. Three are even better, for a triple-braided cord is not easily broken" (Eccl. 4:12 NLT).

We didn't tell many people about our baggage. I had four friends who knew. Who knows about what you are going through? How are they helping you move forward?

Make a list of four people you could reach out to for support and encouragement. Contact them this week.

My husband also had four friends who knew what we were facing. Consider asking your husband to reach out for support and encouragement.

Day 19

Stuck

We have a small lake at the entrance of our neighborhood. It's a wonderful place for boys to explore and get absolutely filthy. One day our son was out playing with some friends. Call it motherly instinct, but I just had a weird feeling. I went outside to get a visual. As I walked around the corner of our house, I was nearly run over by one of my son's buddies. He panted this message:

"Daniel . . . stuck . . . trouble . . . help."

I took off.

When I found Daniel, he was immobile, stuck in the lakeside muck up to his knees, wet to the waist but still standing. I thanked God for the always-on-duty angels who surround this adventurous boy. We struggled and tugged and dug around his wedged-in, water-filled rubber boots, to no avail. With a hefty dose of adrenaline, I grabbed him under the arms and pulled but couldn't break the suction.

"Wiggle your toes!" I yelled, and as I leaned back, finally the suction gave way and he was lifted right out of his boots.

For years I depended on God to help me make it through another day. I wasn't thinking about getting unstuck. I was thinking about survival.

But life is so much more than surviving the struggle.

I could have never left my boy stuck in the muck. I was committed to getting him out of that slimy mess. It didn't matter that I was getting covered in mud. I didn't care how many pairs of shoes we lost to the lake. I wanted my boy free.

Keep Walking

God is here for you today, reaching under your arms to lift you out of the pit and place you on solid ground. Wiggle your toes.

Today I will be lifted out of the pit.

Reflect and Respond:

"He lifted me out of the slimy pit, out of the mud and mire; he set my feet on a rock and gave me a firm place to stand" (Ps. 40:2).

Have you ever been stuck in the mud . . . or even stuck in traffic? In what way do you feel stuck right now?

We lost a perfectly good pair of rubber rain boots to the lake the day Daniel was stuck. It was a small price to pay for freedom. Is there something keeping you stuck that you need to leave behind?

"For he says, 'In the time of my favor I heard you, and in the day of salvation I helped you.' I tell you, now is the time of God's favor, now is the day of salvation" (2 Cor. 6:2).

Don't waste another minute regretting the time you've spent stuck. Today is the day and now is the time. How can you wiggle your toes? What can you do to release yourself from regret and take a step forward today?

While you are thinking about your toes, why not get a pedicure? Pick a vibrant nail color and add some nail art that makes you smile.

Day 20

Revenge

I've never been much for journaling, but I found it incredibly therapeutic during this season of my life. It was a way to clear my head and make space for more rational thoughts.

One day my husband read my journal. No, I didn't "accidentally" leave it out for him to find. He opened documents on my computer and helped himself.

"I suppose I love him, but I don't really have feelings of love anymore."

David was shocked when he read my confession. He had compartmentalized his use of pornography. He believed the lie that it only affected him. My words stung, and when I walked into our home office, he was shattered in tears.

"Just feel it. Feel a little bit of pain. Sit there and soak it up for a while because that's how I feel all the time!" I snarled.

Not my best moment.

I didn't intend to hurt him with my journaling; I never expected him to see it. But I'll admit I was happy to see him suffering. He had caused me more pain that I had ever experienced in my life. It was only fair, right?

We think about revenge because it appeals to our moral conscience. We want payback. It seems like justice.

God says in Deuteronomy 32:35, "Vengeance is mine" (NKJV).

I don't think that verse is a threat; I think it's a word of caution. Steer clear of revenge. God stakes his claim on that. Don't try to inflict it on your own.

Pray and lay that burden down at the foot of the cross.

Keep Walking

Today I release my desire for revenge.

Reflect and Respond:

If you are struggling with thoughts of revenge—desire to see your spouse suffer as you have suffered—please talk to a friend. Ask for accountability.

"Don't insist on getting even; that's not for you to do. 'I'll do the judging,' says God. 'I'll take care of it'" (Rom. 12:19 The Message).

Let's pray: Father, I release my desire for revenge. I abandon any plan I've made to get even. Vengeance is not mine. You are the judge, not I. Help me recognize thoughts of revenge and replace them with thoughts of trusting you. My life is in your hands. My future is in your hands. I am safe with you. You will take care of me.

Buy a journal, or dust off the one you got for Christmas three years ago, or grab an old spiral notebook and spill out your ugly, your worries and your cares in words. Keep it in a safe place.

"Give all your worries and cares to God, for he cares about you" (1 Peter 5:7 NLT).

Day 21

Called to Hope

"God, where are you? I need to see you in this situation!"

I wrestled with God daily over the circumstances of my life. I know I needed to pray but felt like I didn't know what to say or how to say it. The long-term nature of the struggle and the dark reality of what was happening popped the cork of my faith and drained me of hope.

As I searched for words to pray, I remembered Paul's prayers for the Ephesians, and I was grateful to have a template to follow. I echoed his prayer over my life and made it personal by modifying the pronouns:

"I pray that the eyes of [my] heart may be enlightened in order that [I] may know the hope to which he has called [me]" (Eph. 1:18).

Lord, open my eyes. Let me know there is hope. You have called me to hope!

That phrase stopped me: called to hope.

I had always felt this passage indicated that God has a hopeful future for us. But when I prayed it over my life, it seemed like God was calling me to be hopeful, calling me to hope—not in wishing for a distant future but as an action for the moment.

How do I do that when the truth is I'm feeling quite hopeless?

We are called to hope, but we don't have to scrounge it up on our own.

"I pray that God, the source of hope, will fill you completely with joy and peace because you trust in him. Then you will overflow with confident hope through the power of the

Holy Spirit" (Rom. 15:13 NLT).

The God of hope will fill us, and we can overflow with hope, not in our own power or in our own strength but by the power of the Holy Spirit.

Hope is not something we hold or keep bottled up inside. It's meant to be poured out over the circumstances of our lives and the lives of those we love. It's meant to overflow.

Today I will ask God to fill me with hope.

Reflect and Respond:

Do you feel drained of hope? Pray Paul's prayer for the Ephesians for yourself.

"I keep asking that the God of our Lord Jesus Christ, the glorious Father, may give [me] the Spirit of wisdom and revelation, so that [I] may know him better. I pray that the eyes of [my] heart may be enlightened in order that [I] may know the hope to which he has called [me], the riches of his glorious inheritance in his holy people, and his incomparably great power for [I] who believe. That power is the same as the mighty strength he exerted when he raised Christ from the dead and seated him at his right hand in the heavenly realms" (Eph. 1:17–20).

Remember Indiana Jones and his leap of faith in *The Last Crusade*?[7] He made the decision to believe and took a step forward, not knowing the end of the story. Is there an active step of hope you need to take?

"You have made a wide path for my feet to keep them from slipping" (Ps. 18:36 NLT).

Day 22

I Don't Know What to Do

I felt so lost and confused. It was difficult just coming to grips with the reality of my life. I had the strongest sense that I needed to do something. I just didn't know what to do.

One question the counselor repeated often in our sessions was, "What is God telling you to do?"

Not "What is your mother telling you to do?"

Or "What are your friends telling you to do?"

Or "What do you want to do?"

But "What is God telling you to do?"

Maybe your friends and family are gracious and wise. Maybe you are thoughtful and brave. Maybe if you asked your inner circle, "What should I do?" the majority consensus would be helpful. But maybe not.

Regardless of how the other people in your life would direct your decisions, knowing that you are acting in obedience to what God is asking of you brings a whole new level of confidence and calm.

So I take this opportunity today to encourage you to pray and seek, and maybe even fast.

Jehoshaphat was facing a vast army of enemies. Things did not look good. He was alarmed, but he resolved to inquire of the Lord. He proclaimed a fast. He prayed. In 2 Chronicles 20:12 we hear his cry: "'we have no power against this great multitude that is coming against us; nor do we know what to do, but our eyes are upon you'" (NKJV).

I love how he tells it like it is. We are powerless and we don't know what to do. I am challenged and inspired at how he sets his focus and desire for direction on God.

God responds with a plan, and says, "'Do not be afraid or discouraged because of this vast army. For the battle is not yours, but God's'" (2 Chron. 20:15).

I was spent. Tired of pretending. Exhausted from trying to control everything in my life. My familiar coping mechanisms were failing me. I couldn't see a way out of the pain I was experiencing. I couldn't come up with a plan to heal my heart, but God had a plan.

God has a plan for you. Fix your eyes on him. Pray. Seek. Ask. Knock.

Do not be afraid or discouraged. God is with you. He goes before you. He can make a way where there seems to be no way. The battle is not yours, but God's.

He knows what you should do, and he will show you.

Today I will ask God what I should do.

Reflect and Respond:

"Let the morning bring me word of your unfailing love, for I have put my trust in you. Show me the way I should go, for to you I entrust my life" (Ps. 143:8).

Do you already feel like God has given you some instructions? What is one step of obedience you need to take today?

"'Keep on asking, and you will receive what you ask for. Keep on seeking, and you will find. Keep on knocking, and the door will be opened to you. For everyone who asks, receives. Everyone who seeks, finds. And to everyone who knocks, the door will be opened'" (Matt. 7:7–8 NLT).

If you are still waiting for an answer, keep on asking, seeking, and knocking. Be faithful to do what you already know to do. The answer is on the way.

"Whether you turn to the right or to the left, your ears will hear a voice behind you, saying, 'This is the way; walk in it'" (Isa. 30:21).

If your prayer life needs a boost, pick up *The Circle Maker* by Mark Batterson.[8] Write your prayers out on paper. I often find that answers come when I have a piece of notebook paper and a pencil in hand.

Day 23

An Anchor for Your Soul

Our most memorable family vacation took place on Portofino Island in the Florida panhandle with the Gulf of Mexico on one side and the Santa Rosa Sound on the other. We came alive in the bright sunshine and tried every available water sport. One morning my son and I rented stand-up paddleboards. It felt like we were walking on water while schools of fish swam beneath our feet. It was a breathtaking experience in more than one way.

After thirty minutes of beauty and awe, I was breathless from battling the current that had swept us far from shore. We dug our way through the water back toward the beach but made very little progress. When we stopped to rest, any movement we had made toward the shore was lost as the wind and waves pushed us out into open water. Back and forth we struggled until nature won the tug-of-war.

We gave up and flagged down a personal watercraft. They towed us back to the beach, and we collapsed on the sand.

While we were catching our breath, I saw another mom resting, soaking up the sun with her son on a giant air mattress. They were on the same water we just crawled out of, but they looked peaceful and relaxed. They were not carried away by waves. They were carefree.

What did they have that we didn't? An anchor.

Hebrews 6:19 says, "We have this hope as an anchor for the soul, firm and secure."

When we put our hope in a God who heals, restores, and redeems, we are not swept away by the storms of life. Hope in God

53

keeps us from being shipwrecked.

There is hope for you!

Sometimes it's helpful to talk to yourself. It's not silly at all; the psalmist did it all the time. "Why, my soul, are you downcast? Why so disturbed within me? Put your hope in God . . . my Savior" (Ps. 42:11).

Tell yourself to put your hope in God. Let him be your anchor in this storm. Nothing is too hard for him. When life comes crashing in around you, you have a Savior!

Today I will put my hope in God.

Reflect and Respond:

"My soul, wait only upon God *and* silently submit to Him; for my hope *and* expectation are from Him. He only is my Rock and my Salvation; He is my Defense *and* my Fortress, I shall not be moved" (Ps. 62:5–6 AMPC).

Do you know the feeling of being anchored, immovable?

What does it mean to have hope as an anchor?

Let today's affirmation be your self talk today. Write it out on three sticky notes and place them where you will find them throughout the day and in the weeks ahead. "I will put my hope in God."

Day 24

Still Standing

Maybe you feel like giving up, throwing your hands up in defeat and curling up in a corner. Believe me, I've been there. There were days when I lacked both the desire and the determination to stand.

Then along came a song.

Israel Houghton's *Alive in South Africa* project stayed in my CD player for months. It brought a smile to my face and lifted my heart. Over and over I would listen to these songs of hope and freedom. One song in particular, "Still Standing," became my anthem:

You gave me courage to believe
that all your goodness I will see.
and if it had not been for you
standing on my side, where would I be?
If not for your goodness, if not for your grace,
I don't know where I would be today.
If not for your kindness, I never could say,
I'm still standing.
If not for your mercy, if not for your love,
I most likely would have given up.
If not for your favor, I never could say,
I'm still standing but by the grace of God.[9]

Most likely, I would have given up if it had not been for the beautiful grace of God. It's only because of his all-sufficient grace that I was able to stand and withstand this storm in my life. I am still standing. I'm here today reaching out to share the hope and life

I found in him because of his amazing grace.

"But he said to me, 'My grace is sufficient for you, for my power is made perfect in weakness.' Therefore I will boast all the more gladly about my weaknesses, so that Christ's power may rest on me. That is why, for Christ's sake, I delight in weaknesses, in insults, in hardships, in persecutions, in difficulties. For when I am weak, then I am strong" (2 Cor. 12:9–10).

I'm not sure how I feel about boasting in my weakness, but it sounds better than wallowing in my weakness. It sounds like standing. Standing puts me in a position to keep walking.

**Today I will stand in my weakness
and know that God is strong.**

Reflect and Respond:

"So let us come boldly to the throne of our gracious God. There we will receive his mercy, and we will find grace to help us when we need it most" (Heb. 4:16 NLT).

Is there a time of day when you feel a greater need for God's grace? Create a daily calendar reminder with a Scripture or phrase that will remind you to go to God in that moment.

When you want to give up or curl up, stand up instead. Stretch your arms up to the sky. Roll your shoulders back. Hold your head up and use your body to help your mind take on the confident posture of your decision to depend on God's strength in the midst of your weakness. Stay here for a few minutes. Breathe in his grace; it is there to help when you need it most.

Day 25

I'm Not Crazy

I love to put puzzles together. Growing up in North Dakota we called it setting puzzles. It was the perfect way to spend a cold winter evening. I developed a puzzle-setting strategy. First, find the corners and the edge pieces; then work on the bright colors and patterns. Finally, tackle the muted, muddled colors in the middle where you depend more on the shapes of the pieces than on the overall picture to determine where each piece fits. It is so satisfying to put all those little pieces together into one whole picture.

Sometimes the stories of our lives only begin to make sense when we take the time to put the pieces together.

If you've ever stared at the shambles of your life and asked yourself, "Am I crazy?" I have good news for you: crazy people never ask themselves that question.

When I finally owned the reality of my husband's sexual addiction, all the muddled parts of my marriage made sense. It was kind of a relief, like "Phew, I'm not crazy."

My husband was disappointed with me as a young bride. I didn't fix him like he thought I would. I could never be enough for him because lust already had a grip on his mind and lust is never satisfied.

I remember thinking, "Something's not quite right in our home." I was right.

It's not easy to listen to those irrational feelings. Nobody wants to be a conspiracy theorist in her own marriage. We make excuses. We discount our ideas. Sometimes, I think the Holy Spirit is trying to get us to pay attention and we would rather not know.

When you get the feeling that something's not quite right, tune in. Pray. Listen. Maybe it's the missing piece that's been lost under the table stuck in the carpet for months.

The picture may not be tranquil like a Thomas Kinkaid cabin tucked in the woods. It probably won't be playful like Looney Tunes in Santa hats. It could be more like those 3-D pictures from the '90s that you have to stick your nose up to and then back away while looking through the pixilated image, hoping something pops out that makes sense of all the dots and squares and lines and colors. But at least it will be one whole picture.

When God takes the fragmented parts of our lives and brings them together, there may be some pieces that are painful to see, but nothing is wasted in his kingdom.

"When they had all had enough to eat, he said to his disciples, 'Gather the pieces that are left over. Let nothing be wasted'" (John 6:12).

Today I commit to listen to the Holy Spirit inside me.

Reflect and Respond:

"From beginning to end he's there, towering far above everything, everyone. So spacious is he, so roomy, that everything of God finds its proper place in him without crowding. Not only that, but all the broken and dislocated pieces of the universe—people and things, animals and atoms—get properly fixed and fit together in vibrant harmonies, all because of his death, his blood that poured down from the cross" (Col. 1:18–20 The Message).

The disciples were confused, dumbfounded as they watched Jesus die on the cross. His death and all the weird things he said leading up to it only began to make sense in the days and weeks and months that followed. What pieces of your story are beginning to make more sense?

"God, pick up the pieces. Put me back together again. You are my praise!" (Jer. 17:14 The Message).

"God made my life complete when I placed all the pieces before him" (Ps. 18:20 The Message).

Spend some time today laying out the broken pieces of your soul and asking God to pick them up and put you back together. He is a master at making beautiful things out of dust.

Day 26

God Is Not a Man

"'God is not a man, that he should lie, Nor a son of man, that he should repent. Has he said, and will he not do? Or has he spoken, and will he not make it good?'" (Num. 23:19 NKJV).

I've often wondered about this passage. Okay, I wonder about a lot of things in the Bible. Why would God feel the need to highlight this stark comparison and include such a thought in his Word for generations of believers?

I think God needed us to know and remember that he is unlike anyone we experience on this earth. He is not like the men in our lives. He is not like women we know. He is not human. He is completely other.

At the same time, when I read this passage I feel it may be communicating that it *is* human nature to change our minds, to lie in order to avoid consequences and to not keep our costly promises.

I don't mean in any way to normalize betrayal, but somehow this passage helped me understand how my husband could have lived a lie for so long. Human beings have the uncanny ability to do that. I was lying too. I got so good at pretending. No one on the outside looking in had any idea what was happening inside me because the outside seemed quite all right.

It is so easy to lie. Telling the ugly truth can be hard.

Sexual addiction therapists often use polygraph in recovery because addicts become so invested in the life they show the outside world that the truth gets buried even inside their own minds.

It's important to know that when humans are unfaithful or untruthful, God remains utterly faithful, truthful, and constant. Inside, outside and all around, he is the same. He never changes. "'I am the Lord, and I do not change'" (Mal. 3:6 NLT).

You can depend on God. You can lean the whole weight of your soul on him and know you are safe.

Like the storm shelter my brother installed in his Tornado Alley home, God is a strong, safe refuge when everything around you is swirling chaos.

Today I will remember God is not a man.

Reflect and Respond:

"Stop lying to each other; tell the truth, for we are parts of each other and when we lie to each other we are hurting ourselves" (Eph. 4:25 TLB).

Have you been lying too? How are the lies you tell hurting your life?

"Because of the Lord's great love we are not consumed, for his compassions never fail. They are new every morning; great is your faithfulness" (Lam. 3:22–23).

Make a list of the ways you have experienced God's unfailing love and his great faithfulness.

"So God has given both his promise and his oath. These two things are unchangeable because it is impossible for God to lie. Therefore, we who have fled to him for refuge can have great confidence as we hold to the hope that lies before us" (Heb. 6:18 NLT).

"The name of the Lord is a strong tower; the righteous run to it and are safe" (Prov. 18:10 NKJV).

How does God's truthful, unchanging nature help you feel safe?

Day 27

I'm a Mess

A few weeks into therapy I started experiencing chest pain. I went to the doctor and had my heart checked.

"Mrs. Cherry, your heart is perfectly healthy. Are you dealing with any stress in your life right now?"

"Um . . .ya . . . just a little."

As frustrating as it was to deal with chest pain, it was even more irritating to learn this pain in my heart was just the manifestation of what was happening in my head. I almost wished something were physically wrong with me.

I was a mess.

Angry. Ashamed. Afraid.

Burdened. Broken. Betrayed.

Exhausted by the emotional drain and awake in the night with physical pain, I considered medication for anxiety and depression, and I thank God it's available. But with consistent therapy, intentional breathing, and prayer I was able to manage the stress and calm my racing heart.

We tend not to think about breathing because we don't have to. Our brain takes care of it without a conscious thought. When we are stressed, our breath becomes shallow and short. Deep, slow, deliberate breaths calm the body and reduce stress.

Four-square breathing is a simple but effective way to dissipate emotional stress. Here's how:

- Inhale as you count to four.
- Hold for four.

- Exhale as you count to four.
- Hold for four.
- Repeat.

You feel better already, don't you?

Part of the struggle of going through trauma like betrayal is assuming you will always be a mess. But how you feel today is not an indication of all your tomorrows. There is help and hope for you. Keep breathing.

Today I will believe I won't always be such a mess.

Reflect and Respond:

"And me? I'm a mess. I'm nothing and have nothing: make something of me. You can do it; you've got what it takes—but God, don't put it off" (Ps. 40:17 The Message).

Has your physical body exhibited the trauma of betrayal?

When was the last time you scheduled a checkup or saw the dentist or enjoyed a massage? Do something to nurture your health today.

Practice four-square breathing. As you breathe, remember these verses:

"The Lord God formed a man from the dust of the ground and breathed into his nostrils the breath of life, and the man became a living being" (Gen. 2:7).

"Again Jesus said, 'Peace be with you!' . . . And with that he breathed on them and said, 'Receive the Holy Spirit'" (John 20:21–22).

The breath of God is life, peace, and the comfort of the Holy Spirit.

Day 28

Thirsty

I may get myself in trouble, but here I go. I grew up in the frozen tundra of North Dakota. Both of my parents were raised on the farm. When I first moved to the South, I thought, what is the deal with southern girls? They're so touchy and emotional and needy. I'm not like that. I'm a tough northern chick. I don't have needs.

When my husband and I were struggling, the last thing I wanted was to need anything from him. I told myself I didn't need anything from anyone.

Who was I kidding?

When we constantly deny our own needs and those needs aren't getting met, we resign ourselves to a dry, parched existence. Or we find all kinds of destructive ways to slake our thirst.

Our feelings of desperation can either get us into trouble, grasping for whatever we can get our hands on, or they can be the very tool God uses to draw us to him.

The psalmist says, "I spread out my hands to You; My soul longs for You like a thirsty land" (Ps. 143:6 NKJV).

Yes, God uses relationships to meet many of our needs, but he is the only who can satisfy our thirsty souls.

Jesus had a conversation with a very thirsty girl. You may know her as the woman at the well. I don't know why, but when I read her story, I hear her talking with a Jersey accent. Here's my paraphrase:

Jesus asked for some water.

"Are you talkin' ta me? Your people don't usually talk ta my people."

Jesus said, "I can give you living water."

"How you gonna get watah with no containah?"

Jesus was so patient and kind with her. He answered, "Whoever drinks the water I give will never thirst again."

Doesn't that sound good?

The psalmist said, "I thirst for you" (Ps. 63:1). Hundreds of years later Jesus said, "'Come to me and drink'" (John 7:37).

Today I will ask Jesus to satisfy my thirsty soul.

Reflect and Respond:

Are you denying your own needs? Have you resigned yourself to being dry and thirsty?

Would you have the courage to ask someone in your life to meet a need?

Now . . . Close your eyes and imagine a spring of cool, clear, refreshing, life-giving water. Hear it bubbling. Smell the fresh clean scent. See the thick green grass growing all around. Now imagine that water welling up inside of you quenching your deepest thirst.

"'I am about to do something new. It is beginning to happen even now. Don't you see it coming? I am going to make a way for you to go through the desert. I will make streams of water in the dry and empty land'" (Isa. 43:19 NiRV).

Day 29

Be Still

We had a big old Texas thunderstorm one night. I would have slept right through it, but a precious little boy came to my bedside and woke me up.

"I'm scared, Momma, will you snuggle with me?"

I could never say no to an invitation like that. I climbed out of my bed, walked down the hallway, climbed into his, and just held him. I was still a little bigger than he was, so I wrapped him up in my arms and held him close.

The storm raged on. We watched the lightning flash through gaps in the vertical blinds. I didn't say a word. I was just near. That seemed to be enough.

Whenever I'm feeling small, it's good to know there is a God who is bigger than I am, bigger than what I know, bigger than what I see. I need to feel his strong arms holding me.

Thankfully, I don't have to shake and wake him to get his attention in the middle of my storms. He never sleeps (See Ps. 121:4).

I can't stop the storms that roll through our neighborhood in Central Texas. For some reason, although I believe he could have, God didn't still the storms that roared through my life. Instead, he asked me to be still.

"'Be still, and know that I am God'" (Ps. 46:10).

In the stillness I recognize that the God I knew in my pretending was safe and small. The God I came to know through the storm was something else entirely. Just like Lucy's Aslan, as I grew, he grew. "He isn't safe, but he's good."[10]

Through the storm I saw my need for him. I realized I don't

have to rely on my own strength and resolve. I learned to depend on him. I experienced the peace of his presence.

Today I will be still and know that God is God.

Reflect and Respond:

It's easy to use a busy schedule to avoid the thoughts and feelings that come with stillness. Set aside thirty minutes for contemplation free of distraction. Is it hard to be quiet?

What storms are raging inside?

What is the tone of your internal dialogue?

Jesus and his disciples were in a boat when a furious storm arose. The disciples woke Jesus up in a panic. "When Jesus woke up, he rebuked the wind and said to the waves, 'Silence! Be still!' Suddenly the wind stopped, and there was a great calm" (Mark 4:39 NLT).

Paul was a prisoner on a boat when a typhoon blew in. I'm sure Paul had heard the story of how Jesus calmed the storm at sea, and yet Jesus did not calm this storm. Read Acts 27. How do you think Paul felt as he faced this storm? What assurance did he have that God was with him?

What assurance do you have that God is with you in the storm?

Day 30

Come to Me

"'Come to me, all you who are weary and burdened, and I will give you rest. Take my yoke upon you and learn from me, for I am gentle and humble in heart, and you will find rest for your souls. For my yoke is easy and my burden is light'" (Matt. 11:28–30).

The Message says, "Come, walk with me." That is not the same as, "Get up! You need some exercise." No. It's an invitation to intimacy. Hand in hand. Step for step. Conversation. Connection.

Jesus knows weariness is part of our human experience. He doesn't minimize the impact of life's burdens. He simply says, "Come to me. Walk with me."

Some days I didn't feel like taking a single step. Some days I wanted to take one giant leap and leave the mess behind me. Some days I really wanted to run away.

But Jesus called me to walk, to put one foot in front of the other, and move forward in sync with him.

Much of my weariness came from trying to control everything in my life. I wanted to know where my husband was, whom he was with, and what he was looking at. I needed my house clean, the laundry folded, and the boys' fingernails trimmed. I needed them to come when I called and do what I told them to do when I told them to do it. I was carrying the weight of the world on my small shoulders and I found myself exhausted, rubbed raw from pulling on the hard wooden yoke of control.

Jesus invites us to step out of the yoke of control and exchange it for the yoke of trust.

That is beautiful in itself, but he doesn't stop there. He promises rest for our souls. Isn't that where we need rest the most—in that place where our emotions, thoughts, and concerns collide?

I need the easy, breezy, weightless rest that comes from him. I can't get myself to that place without trusting in and partnering with him.

It is freeing to know Jesus understands weariness, burdens, worry, and fear. His invitation is free of condemnation. We don't have to fix ourselves before we come to him. We have a place to go with our burdens. We can drag our heavy old yokes and leave them at his feet.

**Today I will answer Jesus' invitation
to come to him and find rest.**

Reflect and Respond:

"Then the man and his wife heard the sound of the Lord God as he was walking in the garden in the cool of the day" (Gen 3:8).

Adam and Eve heard the sound of God walking in the garden in the cool of the day. I get the feeling this was the routine, a daily opportunity to connect with their Creator.

If you could go for a walk with God, what would you talk about?

Go for a walk with a friend. Notice how you adjust your stride to walk in sync. Is it easier to connect while you are walking?

Are you wearing the yoke of control? How is it wearing you out?

What makes walking with Jesus' yoke lighter?

Day 31

Through

I felt like I was drowning, frantic, arms flailing, reaching for the shore, reaching for something, anything to grab hold of. I slipped under, kicking, stretching, and gasping for air. How much longer can I do this?

Some days were just so hard. I wondered how I was ever going to make it through.

The river of suffering seemed impassable. There was no bridge going over the water and no tunnel going under. I searched for miles down the shore in both directions, but there was no way around this raging river.

"'When you pass through the waters, I will be with you; and when you pass through the rivers, they will not sweep over you. When you walk through the fire, you will not be burned'" (Isa. 43:2).

I grew up in church, and whether I was taught it or just decided it for myself, I believed if I just loved Jesus, I would have an easy life. I wouldn't suffer. Call it Christian karma. But the truth is, God doesn't promise us a life without challenge. There will be deep waters, turbulent rivers, and suffocating flames.

But the key word in this passage is "through."

Would you dare to believe it? You will pass through. You will walk through.

God so sweetly beckoned my broken heart with this verse. Hear him calling you. Just Keep Walkin', Baby. Keep Walking. Keep putting one foot in front of the other. I am right here with you and you will make it through.

Keep Walking

Today I determine to keep walking.

Reflect and Respond:

"Yea, though I walk through the valley of the shadow of death, I will fear no evil; For you are with me; your rod and your staff, they comfort me" (Ps. 23:4 NKVJ).

I love that word "through." Have you set up camp in the valley of the shadow of death? You don't have to stay there! What is one step you can take today toward the other side of suffering?

In the original language the rod and staff are a picture of protection and support. How have you experienced God's presence, protection, support and comfort while you walk through this valley?

Write your own personal version of Psalm 23:4.

Day 32

Trying to Understand

I went on a quest for knowledge as it related to my husband's sexual addiction. I read books. I searched online. I was just trying to understand, trying to make some sense of it all. The statistics were just plain depressing. Still, it helped.

The more I learned, the less isolated I felt.

Truth exposes the lies we believe.

One of the greatest deceptions was believing if I were curvier, sexier, taller, thinner, or just plain more, my husband wouldn't have this problem.

His addiction felt like such a personal rejection. It was not an isolated event but an ongoing whittling away at me. I thought for years it was about me, but now I understand it was a problem before I was even a part of his life. It was never about me, but it did affect me, and I was powerless to fix him.

The most surprising thing about my new knowledge was the compassion I felt for my husband. My self-righteous judgment began to feel more and more uncomfortable.

I could see the need pornography filled in his life. It was a familiar shortcut, a well-worn path he discovered as a boy. It made him feel like he had what it takes to be a man.

As John Eldredge explains in *Wild at Heart*, "What makes pornography so addictive is that more than anything else in a lost man's life, it makes him feel like a man without ever requiring a thing of him."[11]

The shortcut down this dark alley came with collateral damage—my soul. I can't say it made me feel better to understand, but it lifted the burden of blame and responsibility off my shoulders.

If you feel the same urge to understand, you may wish to consult some of these resources that helped me:

- *Harboring Hope,* an online recovery course by Leslie Hardie[12]
- *Living With Your Husband's Secret Wars* by Marsha Means[13]
- *How To Act Right When Your Spouse Acts Wrong* by Leslie Vernick[14]

I'm praying the right resources get in your hands at the right time.

Today I will grab hold of the tools that are put into my hands and begin to do the hard work.

Reflect and Respond:

Read Acts 12:5–10. The story of Peter's release from prison illustrates our part in what God can do. The angel didn't carry Peter out of prison like a sack of potatoes, although I'm sure he could have. Peter had to get up put on his clothes and walk. As Peter did his part, God did what only he can do.

What is your part today? Getting out of bed and taking a shower? Putting on your shoes and going for a walk? Take a step forward today.

"That is why we labor and strive, because we have put our hope in the living God, who is the Savior of all people, and especially of those who believe" (1 Tim. 4:10).

Do your part, but don't place your hope in your ability (or your spouse's ability) to follow a program. How will you remind yourself to keep your hope squarely on the strong shoulders of the Savior?

Day 33

Refreshing

I punched the code in the garage opener keypad, leaning on the doorframe for support. What was I thinking? It was ninety-three degrees, "feels like" ninety-nine when you factor in humidity and yet for some reason, forty-five minutes ago going for a walk in the heat seemed like a good idea.

Yes, a nice long sweat to cleanse all the toxins I ingested while celebrating four birthdays in two weeks was just what I needed.

I went straight to the kitchen and filled a glass of water.

Cool clear hydration. It felt so good, so refreshing going down.

"Like cold water to a weary soul is good news from a distant land" (Prov. 25:25).

I got a cold drink of water from a friend early in our recovery journey. I sat across the table from her and listened to her story. We both cried as she relived the betrayal in her marriage. The tears that flowed carried with them a portion of our shared pain. I drank in revitalizing hope. Even though the wound was still fresh, she had made it through. She got help, did the hard work, and brought good news from a land I longed to live in.

Her news gave me the courage to step away from my familiar coping strategies and move bravely toward that distant land of freedom.

When you are in the middle of a struggle, rest and peace can seem like a faraway place. So when someone shares the hope they've found, it's like cool cucumber water on a hot summer day.

My friend made it through the desert season of her soul. I made it through. You can make it through.

Keep Walking

I pray you are drinking deep dregs of hope as you read these words. May it soak into every dry, shriveled cell and fill it up with new life.

**Today I will drink the refreshing news
of another's restoration story.**

Reflect and Respond:

Is there someone who was courageous enough to share "good news from a distant land" with you? Write them a thank-you note today.

Do you have good news, even a portion of your healing so far, that you could share with someone who is crawling through a desert season? Write her a note or send an encouraging email or text message.

"My mouth will tell of your righteous deeds, of your saving acts all day long—though I know not how to relate them all. I will come and proclaim your mighty acts, Sovereign Lord; I will proclaim your righteous deeds, yours alone. Since my youth, God, you have taught me, and to this day I declare your marvelous deeds. Even when I am old and gray, do not forsake me, my God, till I declare your power to the next generation, your mighty acts to all who are to come" (Ps. 71: 15–18).

Drink a tall glass of pure water. Add a slice of lime or cucumber. If you are used to drinking soda, try switching to sparkling water and be refreshed.

Day 34

Catching My Breath

Fridays were hard. It was our day off, our only day together in the same space without the buffer of two small boys.

We went to therapy on Thursdays, which stirred up all kinds of feelings and fears. The pressure mounted Thursday night, and by Friday morning we were ready to explode.

I would drop the boys off at school and hold my breath on the way home.

Friday was fight day.

We argued about who said what in therapy the day before. We fought over our differing sexual appetites. We circled the same mountain and resurrected past issues as I climbed up on my high horse of self-righteous pride and my husband defended what was left of his dignity.

We poked each other's fresh wounds, slapped sunburned shoulders, and stomped on already broken toes.

I couldn't imagine how we would ever get back to the life we once had together.

And then I remembered a promise in Psalm 23:3 (NKJV): "He restores my soul."

We looked up the words from this passage in the dictionary my husband had just installed on his Palm Pilot (remember those?). The word "restore" was defined as to return to its original, useable, functioning condition. The word "soul" indicated the immaterial part of a person, the activating cause of an individual's life.[15]

God returns our core being to its original functioning condition. That means I don't have to fight for the life I used to have.

Keep Walking

Restoration doesn't mean going back to how things were.

We can't think of restoration as a sloppy DYI home improvement project. A restored soul is not a fresh coat of paint slapped over cracked walls that rest on sloping foundations.

A restored soul is a life completely renovated and returned to its original design, a life we haven't yet imagined.

I love how Eugene Peterson puts it in *The Message*: "True to your word, you let me catch my breath and send me in the right direction."

**Today I will catch my breath
and allow God to restore my soul.**

Reflect and Respond:

Are you fighting with more frequency or intensity and not making any progress toward resolving conflict? Please get help before more damage is done.

"'But I will restore you to health and heal your wounds,' declares the Lord" (Jer. 30:17).

When I read, "He restores my soul," I knew regardless of whether my marriage would be restored, God would restore my soul.

It's cheap and easy to fill cracks in the wall with spackling paste. Foundation repair is costly and time consuming but your soul is worth it. Describe what a restored soul looks like to you. Make a commitment to do the work.

Is there a room in your home that could use some renovation? Refresh the space you live in with colors and textures that make you feel at rest.

Day 35

I Don't Want To

I've never been a morning person. My roommate in college called me the Snooze Queen. But when my life took a downward turn after discovering my husband's addiction, I didn't just hit the snooze button. I turned the alarm off altogether. I didn't want to get up. Getting out of bed felt like moving the Titanic. Sliding out from under the covers to carry the weight of my heavy heart was the biggest hurdle of my day.

I know someone who is experiencing a downward turn of her own. We were talking recently, and like a helpful friend I offered a string of suggestions. Our conversation went something like this:

"Why don't you get outside and go for a walk?."

"I don't want to."

"You could watch a funny movie."

"I don't want to."

"What about taking a bubble bath?"

"I don't want to."

I gave up and left our conversation feeling frustrated. And then I remembered how much I appreciated perky people with helpful suggestions when I had the don't-want-to's.

I always groan whenever someone tells me to turn to Proverbs 31. Seriously, that woman is so annoying. Verse 15 is particularly irritating when you have serious sleeping skills like mine.

"She rises also while it is still night" (Prov. 31:15 NASB).

I'll admit I've made some assumptions about this overachiever. I assume she wants to get up. She's a morning person. But what if my assumption is wrong? What if she rises not because she wants to but because she knows it's the right thing to do? What if she gets up even though she doesn't want to get up at all?

I've learned a few things about desire through the don't-want-to episodes of my life:

- Desire is nice but not necessary.
- If I wait until I want to, I may never take action.
- Doing what I know is good and right, regardless of how I feel, is actually quite satisfying.
- Sometimes the want-to comes after I take the first step.

I'm still not a morning person. Sometimes I leave the blinds open so sunlight will seep in. Nature's alarm clock is the best. Sometimes I let myself linger and read a devotional before getting out of bed. Nowadays I don't let the don't-want-to's keep me under the covers for long.

The Proverbs 31 woman rises. She gets up. She moves forward with or without the want-to—and so do I.

Today I will rise up, with or without the want-to.

Reflect and Respond:

Are you having trouble getting out of bed in the morning? Can you select a friendlier sound for an alarm or pick an uplifting song to wake up to?

If the don't-want-to's keep you down for long, you could be struggling with depression. Ask a professional counselor for help.

"Arise, shine, for your light has come, and the glory of the Lord rises upon you. See, darkness covers the earth and thick darkness is over the peoples, but the Lord rises upon you and his glory appears over you" (Isa. 60:1–2).

Aside from getting out of bed in the morning, in what way do you need to rise up?

Day 36

Relearning

My youngest learned to hold a pencil the way you'd grip a handlebar. He wrapped all his chubby fingers around the barrel, tilted his wrist and chicken-scratched his way through pre-K. When his teacher and I discovered what he had learned, we began the arduous process of helping him relearn a proper pencil grip.

It is much easier to learn than to relearn.

There are a few passages of Scripture I had to relearn as I walked through this difficult season.

"'The thief comes only to steal and kill and destroy; I have come that they may have life, and have it to the full'" (John 10:10).

I like the part about life, abundant life. Doesn't that sound lovely?

What I've had to relearn is "the thief comes." I think I usually skipped that part or at the very least decided it didn't apply to me.

But there is an enemy of our soul who comes at our lives with determined focus. You may feel like the life you once knew was stolen right out of your hands. You may feel like you're dying. It may look like your life is lying in shambles around you, but in the middle of the devastation Jesus comes with rich, full life.

Here's another verse I had to relearn:

"I have told you these things, so that in me you may have peace. In this world you will have trouble. But take heart! I have overcome the world" (John 16:33).

I would prefer to have my peace in the absence of trouble, thank you very much.

This peace is different. It's peace in the presence of trouble.

I grew up believing if I just loved Jesus, I could escape trouble altogether. But Jesus never promised me that kind of life.

What he did promise is our trouble-stained, sin-soiled lives on this planet are not too much for him. I don't often appreciate God's willingness to allow difficulty in my life, but I am relearning the truth that no matter what comes my way, he is with me. He never abandons me in the trouble. It's not too much for him. He has overcome the world. He redeems the destruction. He transforms the trouble.

**Today I will believe the trouble I'm facing
is not too much for God.**

Reflect and Respond:

What evidence have you seen of the thief's plot to steal, kill, and destroy?

Is there anything you are relearning about God? The Bible? Faith?

"'Be strong and courageous. Do not be afraid or terrified because of them, for the Lord your God goes with you; he will never leave you nor forsake you'" (Deut. 31:6).

How does knowing that God is always with you prepare you for challenging circumstances?

In what way are you experiencing life and peace in the middle of trouble?

"Do not be anxious about anything, but in every situation, by prayer and petition, with thanksgiving, present your requests to God. And the peace of God, which transcends all understanding, will guard your hearts and your minds in Christ Jesus" (Phil. 4:6–7).

Write a prayer inviting God into your trouble and asking for his peace.

Day 37

You Want Me to What?

You want me to forgive? I'm not sure I can do that. Forgiveness feels like lying naked on the cold tile and saying, "Sure, I'll be your doormat. Go ahead and walk all over me. Scrape your dirty shoes back and forth across my chest. Do it again tomorrow and the next day. It's all good."

But choosing to forgive is not surrendering to mistreatment. Forgiveness is not a submission of the weak; it is a decision of the strong.

In her transformational book *Strong Women, Soft Hearts: A Woman's Guide to Cultivating a Wise Heart and a Passionate Life,* Paula Rinehart has this to say about the demands of forgiveness of this magnitude:

"Forgiving the day-to-day slights and irritations that come your way is small potatoes compared to the work of forgiving serious injury from another person—of feeling betrayed by someone you love. The everyday stuff is what the Bible simply calls "bearing with" someone. But when the hurt has been costly and you may feel the impact for years to come—well, that is like getting a graduate degree in forgiveness."[16]

My friend is getting her master's degree. The work is intense. She labors over each paper and project. She spent four hours on the phone one day with technical support trying to upload a presentation before the deadline. She slogged through computer glitches, programming errors, and misleading information to get it in on time. It required persistent dedication and focused determination.

Getting a graduate degree in forgiveness is arduous, repetitive work.

Early in the work I didn't want to forgive because I didn't want to get hurt again. Unforgiveness guaranteed a safer distance between us. Later in the work I was afraid to forgive because I felt like I would have to pretend I was okay with what happened, and I was not okay.

But forgiveness doesn't mean reconciliation, and it doesn't condone what happened. It doesn't guarantee I won't be hurt again, and it doesn't mean I'm ready to trust my heart. Forgiveness isn't about my betrayer; it's about me.

Forgiveness is the key that unlocks the prison doors of pain.

Forgiveness means I get to move forward.

Today I will make a choice to forgive.

Reflect and Respond:

I was so relieved when I read Paula Rinehart's words about graduate-level forgiveness. It felt like someone was acknowledging for the first time how difficult it can be to forgive. Is it difficult for you to forgive? Why are you reluctant?

"Bear with each other and forgive one another if any of you has a grievance against someone. Forgive as the Lord forgave you" (Col. 3:13).

When has another person had to "bear with" you?

Have you ever been forgiven at the graduate level?

How does knowing you've been forgiven help you choose to forgive?

In his book *Stop Sex Addiction: Real Hope, True Freedom for Sex Addicts and Partners*, Dr. Milton Magness warns against premature forgiveness when it comes to sex addiction.[17] For some addicts, hearing the words "I forgive you" can feel like resolution. They may resist questions or further discussion of any issue under the umbrella of forgiveness. If you are dealing with sexual addiction, know that you can make a choice to forgive, but you may need to wait to express forgiveness to your partner. Talk to a therapist who specializes in sexual addiction if you are struggling with when to offer forgiveness.

Day 38

Give Them Up

"'I will say to the north, "Give them up!" and to the south, "Do not hold them back." Bring my sons from afar and my daughters from the ends of the earth'" (Isa. 43:6).

As I was reading Isaiah's prophecy, I felt like it was a timely word for those who feel trapped, stuck, or bound in the pain of betrayal.

Hear God saying this to whatever is holding you:

Give them up, rejection.

Don't hold them back, addiction.

Give them up, shame.

Don't hold them back, pain.

Give them up, loneliness.

Don't hold them back, depression.

Give them up, anxiety.

Don't hold them back, fear.

Give them up, _____.

Don't hold them back, _____.

Release my sons and daughters!

God wants us to live and walk in freedom. It's why Jesus came. Isaiah also prophesied about Jesus' work on the earth. One day Jesus read his prophesy and told everyone gathered around that Isaiah's words had come to life that day. I think of it as Jesus' personal mission statement.

"The Spirit of the Lord is on me, because he has anointed me to proclaim good news to the poor. He has sent me to proclaim freedom for the prisoners and recovery of sight for the blind, to set the oppressed free" (Luke 4:18).

Freedom!

Our part is to process the pain. We do have to own our story. Just don't cling to it. Don't allow it to define you. Know that God is speaking these words of freedom over you.

Today I will believe for freedom.

Reflect and Respond:

What has you bound? What is holding you back?

Write a freedom proclamation. Give me up, _____! Do not hold me back, _____!

"It is for freedom that Christ has set us free. Stand firm, then, and do not let yourselves be burdened again by a yoke of slavery" (Gal. 5:1).

Jesus set us free from the things that bind us. Our freedom is for a purpose. What are you free for?

Day 39

Trust in God

In Jeremiah 17 we find two distinct approaches to life: one that trusts in self and one that trusts in God. When I read about the two women in this passage, I knew I had a choice to make. Here is my paraphrase of verses 5 and 6:

The woman who trusts in her own flesh, in her own plan, is cursed. She is lonely because she sees nothing but herself. She misses out on the good things in life, completely unaware of her blessings. She lives in a hard, desolate place. She is dry and brittle, so she snaps under pressure. (Been there, done that.) Like the children of Israel in the desert, she keeps going around in circles, taking forty years to make a several-day journey. She lives a lifeless existence. Nothing grows around her or in her.

Sadly, I have lived those verses. Have you?

Here's the good news: there's an alternative in verses 7 and 8. We see a completely different picture of a completely different girl. Here is my paraphrase:

The woman who trusts in God is blessed! She is full of life. She is cared for, intended, planted in a specific place where life-giving water flows with provision. She does not live in fear of the pain life brings. She is confident to face adversity. She knows God is a redeemer. His breath is life. She is beautiful, green, nourished—alive! She will not be anxious in dry seasons because she knows who she is and whom she belongs to. Her roots go deep to hidden stores and resources. She is always fruitful, able to bear fruit in any season, because her source of life is deeper than what the weather may bring.

Keep Walking

Today I choose to put my trust in God.

Reflect and Respond:

Apply the following passage to your story. Write your own personal paraphrase of verses 5 and 6.

"'Cursed is the one who trusts in man, who draws strength from mere flesh and whose heart turns away from the Lord. That person will be like a bush in the wastelands; they will not see prosperity when it comes. They will dwell in the parched places of the desert, in a salt land where no one lives'" (Jer. 17:5–6).

Now paraphrase verses 7 and 8.

"'But blessed is the one who trusts in the Lord, whose confidence is in him. They will be like a tree planted by the water that sends out its roots by the stream. It does not fear when heat comes; its leaves are always green. It has no worries in a year of drought and never fails to bear fruit'" (Jer. 17:7–8).

Find an image that could represent or symbolize the woman you see in verses 7 and 8. Draw, paint, or google and print. Let it inspire you to abandon trusting in your own strength and choose to trust in the Lord.

Day 40

Truth Brings Freedom

"Love . . . rejoices in the truth" (1 Cor. 13:4 –6 NKJV).

WHAT?

How could love possibly rejoice in the painful truth of my life?

Honestly when I ran across this verse, it just made me so mad. It's a good thing I read my Bible with a highlighter in hand and not a permanent marker.

The truth of my life was ugly and shameful. Owning the truth caused great pain. How on earth could love rejoice in that? How is it even possible?

God gently reminded me of another verse in John 8:32: "'Then you will know the truth, and the truth will set you free.'"

Love rejoices because it knows the truth is not an end in itself.

Knowing the truth is the beginning of freedom.

I believe with all my heart there is freedom in knowing the truth even when the truth has left an ugly mark on our lives.

When we stop pretending and acknowledge what is going on inside of us or in our world, then Jesus who is "the truth" will set us free from living a life where we continue to carry around the weight of our pain.

We are free to lift our hands. Free to get out of bed. Free to love and laugh again. Free to put one foot in front of the other. Free to keep walking.

It feels good to be free.

Today I will embrace freedom.
I will move forward. I will keep walking.

Reflect and Respond:

"But I trust in your unfailing love; my heart rejoices in your salvation" (Ps. 13:5).

Go for a walk and reflect on the courage you've discovered and the freedom you have found over the past forty days.

"I'm not trying to get my way in the world's way. I'm trying to get your way, your Word's way. I'm staying on your trail; I'm putting one foot in front of the other. I'm not giving up" (Ps. 17:4–5 The Message).

Dedication

This book is dedicated to my courageous husband, David, who not only shares his story, but encourages me to share mine. I'm so glad we made our way through that dark part in the middle of our story together.

How to Connect with Lynn

Visit LynnMarieCherry.com

"Like" Lynn's author page on Facebook
https://www.facebook.com/keepwalkingbook/

Follow on Twitter
@LynnMarieCherry

Follow on Instagram
@LynnMarieCherry

For updates on future books,
sign up for the Keep Walking Newsletter
http://eepurl.com/b8z0cL

♥|✚ affair recovery

It's not as hopeless as it feels.

For Betrayed Spouses	For Couples
Harboring Hope	**EMS Online**
Choose hope for yourself. This 13 week course will serve as your travel guide through the pitfalls and hardships of rescuing yourself from the pain of betrayal. Join 5 other betrayed women and walk with them towards healing and finally breathe again.	Commit to seeing what's worth salvaging, even if you can't commit to one another just yet. In 13 weeks, learn how you and your spouse got to this place, how to heal now that you're here, and how to keep from returning. Develop the intimate, secure, and loving marriage you've always wanted.

To learn more visit www.AffairRecovery.com

Notes

1. Ann Voskamp, *One Thousand Gifts: A Dare to Live Fully Right Where You Are* (Grand Rapids, MI: Zondervan, 2010)

2. *The Princess Bride* Dir. Rob Reiner, Perf. Billy Crystal. Twentieth Century Fox Film Corp., 1987. Film.

3. Beth Moore, *When Godly People Do Ungodly Things: Arming Yourself in the Age of Seduction* (Nashville, TN: Broadman & Holman, 2002)

4. *A Thousand Clowns* Dir. Fred Coe, Writer Herb Gardner, Perf. Jason Robards, United Artists, 1965. Film

5. Dr. Gloria Wilcox, *Feelings: Converting Negatives to Positives* (Morris Publishing, 2001) This book is currently out of print but you can find an image of the feelings wheel online

6. Elisabeth Kübler-Ross and David Kessler. *On Grief and Grieving: Finding the Meaning of Grief through the Five Stages of Loss* (New York: Scribner, 2005)

7. *Indiana Jones and the Last Crusade.* Dir. Steven Spielberg. Perf. Harrison Ford Paramount Pictures, 1989.

8. Mark Batterson, *The Circle Maker: Praying Circles around Your Biggest Dreams and Greatest Fears* (Grand Rapids, MI: Zondervan, 2011)

9. *Still Standing* Cindy Cruse Ratcliff and Israel Houghton Integrity's Praise! Music, My Other Publishing Company, Sound Of The New Breed 2005 Used with Permission

10. C.S. Lewis, *The Chronicles of Narnia: The Signature Edition* (New York: Harper Collins Publishers, 2006) *Prince Caspian*, 380, *The Lion, the Witch and the Wardrobe* 146

11. John Eldredge, *Wild at Heart: Discovering the Passionate Soul of a Man* (Nashville, TN: T. Nelson, 2001) 44

12. Leslie Hardie, *Harboring Hope Online Recovery Course* https://www.affairrecovery.com/product/harboring-hope

13. Marsha Means, *Living with Your Husband's Secret Wars* (Grand Rapids, MI:

F.H. Revell, 1999)

14. Leslie Vernick, *How to Act Right When Your Spouse Acts Wrong* (Colorado Springs: Waterbrook Press, 2001)

15. David's Palm Pilot is long gone. I am not able to confirm the exact source of these definitions and am quoting an email I sent to our recovery group in which I originally shared the information. However, the definitions are almost identical to those in the *Merriam-Webster Dictionary* and there was a version available for the Palm.

16. Paula Rinehart, *Strong Women Soft Hearts, A Woman's Guide to Cultivating a Wise Heart and a Passionate Life* (Nashville: Word Pub., 2001) 116

17. Milton S. Magness *Stop Sex Addiction: Real Hope, True Freedom for Sex Addicts and Partners* (Las Vegas: Central Recovery Press, 2013) 172-174

Made in the USA
Middletown, DE
12 May 2020